YOGA BEGINNER

Basic Poses You Need to Know as a Beginner

Tips on Easy Weight Loss Exercises that Help Limit Stress and Pain, First Steps through Meditation and the Benefits of Yoga in Your Life

by

Anna Shine

The information provided herein is stated to be truthful and consistent, in that any liability, in terms of inattention or otherwise, by any usage or abuse of any policies, processes, or directions contained within is the solitary and utter responsibility of the recipient reader. Under no circumstances will any legal responsibility or blame be held against the publisher for any reparation, damages, or monetary loss due to the information herein, either directly or indirectly. Respective authors own all copyrights not held by the publisher.

The information herein is offered for informational purposes solely and is universal as so. The presentation of the information is without the contract or any type of guarantee assurance.

The trademarks that are used are without any consent, and the publication of the trademark is without permission or backing by the trademark owner. All trademarks and brands within this book are for clarifying purposes only and are the owned by the owners themselves, not affiliated with this document.

Contents

Introduction

Thank you for making the right decision to read this wonderful and informative book about yoga and meditation. It shows you are on the right track to get your body, mind, and spirit in shape so you can tackle the good and bad that life has in store for you with all your potential.

Before we begin with the yoga and exploring a portion of this vast sea, let us for a moment understand the beauty and powers of our mind. Yoga, after all, is an exercise of our mind as much as of our body.

H. E. Davey has quoted the following:

"A positive attitude is most easily arrived at through a deliberate and rational analysis of what's required to manifest unwavering positive thought patterns. First, reflect on the actual, present condition of your mind. In other words, is the mind positive or not? We've all met individuals who perceive themselves as positive people but don't appear as such. Since the mind is both invisible and intangible, it's, therefore, easier to see the accurate characteristics of the mind through a person's words, deeds, and posture.

For example, if we say, 'It's absolutely freezing today! I'll probably catch a cold before the end of the day!' then our words express a negative attitude. But if we say, 'The temperature is very cold' (a simple statement of fact), then our expressions, and therefore attitude, are not negative. Sustaining an alert state in which self-awareness becomes possible gives us a chance to discover the origins of negativity. In doing so, we also have an opportunity to arrive at a state of positiveness, so that our words and deeds are also positive, making others feel comfortable, cheerful, and inspired."

Now that you have read about the connection between our minds and our bodies, wouldn't you like to prepare yourself both mentally and physically to improve the way you function and interact with other people? This book is especially for those who are in pursuit of the yoga and meditation-based exercises to strengthen their minds and bodies to improve the quality of their lives. Once you work your inner and outer self, you automatically start functioning in a better manner and people look at you differently. All you need to do is make up your mind and gear up your body to follow the simple but very powerful steps of yoga and meditation to work on all aspects of your life and your body.

It has been proven several times by various people that meditation and yoga can be accredited with wonderful changes in a person's body and mind, so much so that they are almost considered miraculous! By reading this book, you are unlocking the chest to a treasure which will help you get started with these steps easily and immediately at your home. If you are worried about not being able to deal with them because of a hectic work schedule, then don't worry – there are plenty of options for you to try at your workplace too. And the best part is, with yoga and meditation, you don't need to have a bunch of fancy equipments or a well-equipped place. You don't need to spend hours punishing your body to become better. You can instead practise these routines in a short span of time with minimum of fuss space and equipment-wise.

So read on to know more about what yoga postures you can practise, how you can kick-start an effective meditation routine and why you should be making such changes in your life!

The Ideology of Yoga

When it comes to discussing yoga, many can find the subject matter a little baffling – just what constitutes yoga? Is yoga a religion? The ideology of yoga itself is a hard thing to pinpoint, but its rich and unique history is very much worth knowing about if you want to better your quality of life for the years to come.

The majority of people look at meditation and yoga, and see it as some form of comical religion that people are falsely believing in. these are people who have never tried yoga.

Whilst yoga has been used for close to 10,000 years – maybe even longer – modern yoga has been a massive help to many people as it has become a topic which is less focused in just the eastern part of the world and has become more westernised as time has gone on. Modern yoga comes from the late 1800s into the early 1900s, as it began to circulate into western culture and become even more powerful.

The first major usage of western yoga comes from the Parliament of Religions, Chicago, in 1893. Swami Vivekananda showed the audience a stunning lecture on yoga, and showing them how it can be a universal thing. By the 1930s, many forms of yoga were being practices as it began to spread all across the world. People like BKS Iyengar, TKV Desikachar and PattabhiJois started to spread the qualities of yoga across the world and before long it has become a major, telling part of society as a whole.

It was not until Indra Devi opened her first yoga studio in Hollywood, in 1947 that things started to radically change and alter to fit the modern world. Since then, many western and Indian people have become genuine pioneers of meditation and yoga, showcasing its immense qualities all across the world. Yoga now has millions of followers and active practitioners, with many schools of thought existing and many different ways of managing yoga.

The best part? Most of these schools of thought are perfectly legitimate and will give you a full and total understanding of the immense power that yoga olds in the right hands.

Meditation

Meditation has, for some time now, been one of the major elements of spiritual success, control and guidance. It's a genuinely pre-historic subject that has been found throughout history in numerous different forms and methods as time has progressed. In truth, having an exact detail for when – or where – meditation first became a thing is nearly impossible.

For anyone who wishes to try and find the very first origins of the power of meditation, you might be waiting for some time! One of the most effective ways to make the most of meditation, though, is to understand the various effects that it can have.

The earliest written records of meditation, known then as Dhyana, came from old Vedantism-based Hindus as far back as 1,500 BCE. At this time, the Vedas discussed the meditative tradition of ancient

India and by the 5th century BCE, Taoist Chinese and Buddhist Indians had appeared and brought their own form of meditation to the table.

Early Buddhism took on the major influence of Vedanta by the 4th century and since then it has become a much muddier road to understand just how meditation continued to change. Buddhist meditation is a subject of immense debate as written records show various different ideologies and facts, so finding a definite answer on this is very hard.

However, the history of meditation in the modern world is far clearer. By the 18th century, Buddhism in the West had become a major topic of study as people wished to better understand other parts of the world.

People like Schopenhauer made regular discussions about the topic a thing of normality, and the likes of Voltaire asked for total tolerance towards Buddhists. The first translation of the Boko of the

Dead, a vital tome in Tibetan culture and history, was published in 1927.

Many new schools of yoga have popped up over the years, as well, developed in Hindu revivalism cultures in the late 1800s. Some of these schools were introduced to western culture by the likes of Vivekananda and other late gurus of the art of meditation. Many schools began to bring together many yoga traditions so that non-Hindus could get involved with the idea of meditation without having to be devout in religion.

The likes of Hatha Yoga became extremely popular as did Transcendental Meditation. Before long it was these ideas that held the most prevalence in the west as people became entranced by the idea of "Yoga" rather than any of its particular schools of thoughts or ideologies. It was this major change in thinking that led to some massive changes later.

The Seven Basic Chakra

All of our bodies have seven special chakra that run through our centres, which energy literally flows through and empowers us. Understanding the immense power of your chakra is a hard thing, and something that many people can struggle to understand and capitalize on in their lives. The chakra that you need to understand how to utilize and understand, though, are;

The Root – This is our very foundations and the feeling of being grounded. It's at the base of the spine, around the tailbone, and acts on survival instincts such as knowing we have money and food. This is the very basis for our emotional wellbeing otherwise, making it a deeply powerful feeling that has to be utilized and controlled to get the best out of ourselves.

The Sacrral – The Sacral Chakra is another important system to manage and learn about in the mind, as it is our vital connection to accept others and enjoying new experiences. This is located in the lower abdomen and tends to give us a feeling of person pleasure and well-being.

Solar Plexus – This is our ability to feel in control of our lives and it sits within the upper abdomen. This gives us important emotional feelings such as self-worth and helps us manage vital elements of our belief system such as how we feel about ourselves otherwise.

The Heart – The Heart Chakra is probably one of the most challenging parts of the mind to get around and understand, mainly as this is genuinely our ability to love. Without this being in connection with one another we can struggle to feel that important inner peace that makes life so much simpler. We also lack important feelings such as empathy, love and joy.

The Throat – The Throat Chakra is one that allows us to genuinely communicate with others. Without that we would lack the strength of character and the ability to communicate with others. When this Chakra is blocked we struggle to put our own opinions and beliefs across to others, and struggle to either tell or understand what the truth entails for us. This is a deeply important Chakra, and one that will affect your entire life without close management.

Third Eye – The Third Eye Chakra is one of the most important, and it is our ability to focus on the bigger picture within our lives. This means that we have the ability to imagine things and to lay out, in our minds, what the potential outcome of something may be. This is very important as it will help you fully understand your emotional issues as well as the ability to create and understand any wisdom that was sent to you. At the very base of its powers and its strengths, this is the ability to think critically and to make major decisions in our lives

– the kind of decisions that we otherwise would never have tried to make anyway.

Crown – The Crown Chakra is another major part of the body and the mind, and something that you should definitely try and understand. The highest of all the Chakra, this works on our ability to be connected spiritually and to fully understand the nature of our lives in many different ways. It's connected to both inner and outer beauty as well as our connection to a strong level of spirituality and beyond.

Each Chakra is well worth exploring further, as they help you understand the connection in the mind with how we feel on so many different levels throughout our lives.

The Benefits of Meditation

Meditation comes with many benefits which are worth knowing about and understanding, specifically as they help to show people the immense power that something as emotionally enriching as meditation can bring to the table. For just some of the ideas of what meditation is capable of bringing to the table, consider that meditation can help with the following;

Removes stress from the body and makes you far more likely to feel at home within yourself, allowing you to rid the mind of fears that you should never have been carrying in the first place. Stress removal is one of the most common reasons why people get involved with yoga and meditation anyway.

Reduces the aging process, too, as your body spends less time fighting against itself and more time worrying about matters that it can deal with and understand. Meditation allows us to calm ourselves in various ways within the mind, and this is captures perfectly with aging.

Adds more time to the day as you spend more time being organized and being in sync with what you need to know and understand about any given day. This is a major feature and one that can more or less transform lives, making you feel far more secure within the realms of your own mind.

Increases your attention span as you are less distracted mentally, making it much easier for you to enjoy and engage with yourself in the years to come. Ensures that you will be more likely to stay in line with the train of thought you had.

Helps you appreciate your life more than ever as it gives you a greater appreciation of the real things in life. Instead of worrying about materialism or things that don't actually matter all that much, you will find that life is much easier to appreciate when you only concentrate on the things that genuinely do matter to you.

This in turn will help you feel far more connected to the world as a whole and much more likely to deal with problems and to handle solutions as time moves on, helping you feel at peace with your mind and your spirit.

Makes you feel happier in numerous ways but also helps you pass on that happiness to others, as you will be a more caring and giving individual.

Improves brain function so you can attack your day instead of just plodding along. It makes a huge difference to your overall mentality and your motivation in so many different aspects, changing how you feel about your life in many ways.

Helps to increase immunity within the body so that you can fight back against disease and illness for many more years to come in your own way.
And much more!

Famous Users of Meditation

Meditation is not just used by experts, it has become the realm of choice for people in positions of power, fame and celebrity. From the late Steve Jobs to people like Arianna Huffington right through to the likes of Kobe Bryant, many people engage with meditation to better their lives in many different ways.

The best way to understand meditation? Listen to the Beatles star, Sir Paul McCartney;

"In moments of madness, meditation has helped me find moments of serenity — and I would like to think that it would help provide young people a quiet haven in a not-so-quiet world."Sir Paul McCartney

"Yoga is the unifying art of transforming dharma into action, be it through inspired thought,

properly nurturing our children, a painting,
a kindness or an act of peace that forever moves
humanity forward. " Micheline Berry

The Yoga Diet

Many people will have heard the term "The Yoga Diet" and probably been a little confused – why would a meditative ideology come with its own diet? Surely you don't have to eat a specific way to get the best out of yoga?

Well, you don't **have to** eat a certain way to get the full benefits of yoga. What you do need to do, though, is eat the right way. That is all the yoga diet is – the specific nature of it only exists because there are simply too many foods to pick from that are good for us. This diet, then, acts as the easiest way possible to discover the foods that are going to serve you best in the weeks, months and years to come.

The Yoga Diet, otherwise known as the Yogic Diet, is a hugely powerful solution for those who enjoy a diet which is made us of foods like dairy products, fruits, nuts, vegetables, grains and legumes. All of these foods are very good for you as they tend to be whole, they tend to be fresh and best of all they don't be unprocessed. The end result?A happy body and a healthy look.

The Yogic Diet was actually thought up by Yogi Bhajan, who wanted to ensure that his students would be taking in the right quality of food as much as anything else.

With no eggs, poultry, fish or meat involved many people might recoil in fear. You can get all of the vitamins and minerals that you need without meat, though, so many people are unsure of what direction they wish to go down with regards to this kind of diet. Are they willing to sacrifice the "good" taste of all that meat in exchange for getting the same nutritional value elsewhere?

If you are then you are in the right place. The only reason that dairy products are on our list, by the way, is because they help you create more mucus. Many of the yogic activities will remove mucus from the body and whilst this is normally a good thing, we need some to keep our breathing passages well lubricated.

The Three Disciplines

For anyone who wants to take the Yogic Diet as serious as they can, you need to understand the three major disciplines;

Sattvic– for those who live a quiet and simple life. The majority of this are "sun foods" such as fruit and vegetables.

Rajasic – for those involved in demanding lifestyles such as taking on serious martial arts. Rajasic lifestyles tend to use spices and herbs, mostly foods from the earth.

Tamasic – for those who lead an impulsive life. Tends to be full of the things we want to avoid like meat, fish, poultry, drink and drugs.

Of course, the last of the disciplines is the one we wish to avoid. Many people therefore live like a balance of the first two and pick or choose the best parts from that to try and build their dietary choices around. After all, you are what you eat in this world and for many people that can be the most important thing to grasp and get their heads around; the food that you ingest directly decides how you feel the next day.

Live a life of cheap meat and drugs? Then you'll feel it every morning. If you live a life using the foods above – and below – you'll find that life is much easier to live through.

Suggested Meals

One of the best parts about general life is that you can always find some solutions for the problems that you face today. How do you sort this? It's actually relatively simple. Start off by checking out the Yoga Journal as they provide daily updates on some of the best recipes to look into, but we also suggest that as a starter you consider any of the following;

Any **fruits** which are naturally sweet – you can find a great selection of fruits to eat in this way. Few things start you off in the day as powerfully as going for some fruit in this manner. It will make a fairly telling difference to the level of enjoyment and class that you get from your foods.

All **vegetables** bar onion and garlic. Both will cause significant issues not only with your breath, but with the kind of foods that we want to take in. Try and avoid anything outside of this.

Whole grains such as **oats**, wheat and **rice** are another product that you will want to keep an eye on so make sure that you take both of these products into account when you are moving forward with your diets.

Beans, **tofu** and aduki are all very good for the body and provide you with plenty of the nutrients that you would normally expect to have in the body anyway.

Natural, raw sugar such as **molasses** or maple will be a good way to give your body the sweetness it needs without resorting to the processed muck.

Use plant-based oils on your foods like **sunflower, olive and sesame oil** to see a nice uptake in the quality, taste and healthiness of your foods.

Herbal teas such as water with lime or lemon in there to add a nice health kick as well as some genuinely enjoyable flavour.

Sweet spices such as **cinnamon, mint, basil and turmeric** all make a big difference to how you feel and how you think – make the most of that if you can as they are readily available.

Make sure that you do some looking around and research into **various foods** you may never have tried before. A bit of exploration and management with your food does genuinely go a pretty long way in this world, so be sure to take the time to try it out and see what you think – experimentation will make such a massive difference later on for you.

Basic Yoga Postures or Asanas

Yoga postures, traditionally known as asanas, have been decided upon by ancient scholars of India to help treat various parts of your body and mind. Some of them are complicated but overall, there are several simple asanas too that you can get started with. Even though these may seem very simple to you, they are in fact very powerful poses that your body is assuming because there are a lot of internal benefits that your body and mind gain. So even if you don't see any apparent external changes immediately, don't give up on your routine because asanas work slowly but steadily and their effects will last you for a very, very long time.

Getting started with Yoga

Before we begin with describing the various asanas or poses that you can start off with, here are a few basic things that you need to stock up on so that you can carry out your yoga asanas with ease and correctly.

1. **A clean mat** - There are several brands of yoga mats that are easily available in the market. Not only do they look trendy, they are also very easily portable and can be rolled up and stored when not in use. They will not occupy a lot of space so you can stash it in your big tote or even in your office so you can be yoga-ready at anytime, anywhere.

2. **A timer** – There are various asanas or poses that only need to be held for a few minutes at a time. There are repetitive sets of some asanas that you may have to do. Instead of over or under-exercising your body, it would be best to start off with a timer, at least until you are familiar with the process and can time yourself reasonably accurately.

3. **Comfortable clothes** – By this, you don't have to splurge on those tight or designer or really short tights and tank tops that many people falsely claim

are yoga clothes. It is preferable you wear separates – tops and bottoms, and you keep them reasonably well-fitted. It is important to let your skin breathe and blood flow within all parts of your body, uninterrupted. Tight, uncomfortable clothes will hamper blood circulation which can lead to disastrous results. Moreover, you will not be able to fully extend your arms or legs in ill-fitting clothes. On the other hand, wearing extremely loose clothes will also get you tangled up and unable to correctly form important or complicated poses. Also, please ensure you do not wear socks or shoes while doing yoga.

4. **Other physical attributes** – Keep yourself well-nourished before you start your yoga session. It means you keep yourself satiated without gorging on too much food or starving yourself for the sake of those complicated asanas. Keep yourself as free as possible from jewellery, hair falling all over your face or body, accessories and other personal items that you normal use when you are about to

step out of your house. Keep yourself as loose, limber and natural as possible. Keeping yourself well hydrated is also very important; it will help loosen up some of those muscles and tendons.

5. **Time** – There is no specified time to perform yoga. While some people argue it is best to do yoga at the crack of dawn, some people find it useful to do it at their convenience during any time of the day. The best way to answer this question is to fully understand the type of asana that you are going to perform because some of them do have time specifications. For example, the Surya Namaskar, which is also a salutation to the Sun God, is best performed early in the morning when the sun is rising. There are some asanas that can be done during any time of the day and at any place, provided your body is in the required state. For example – some asanas are to be performed only when a few hours have passed your last meal while some require you to be just about to hit the bed.

6. **Ambience** – If you want to encourage yourself to remain interested and focussed on the task at hand, you can enhance the mood by using soft, classical Indian music, preferably only instrumental, in the background. Placing idols of pictures of Gods and Goddesses to channel the inner spiritualism within you is also a good idea if you are amiable to do so. You could also arrange for suitable lighting and some incense sticks. Anything that will keep you calm and a place where you can be least or not at all distracted would provide the best ambience.

7. **Breathing** – Practise on your inhalation and exhalation patterns. Both yoga and meditation place a lot of importance on the way you draw in and let out your breath because they play a vital role in the way your mind works, your muscles react and blood circulates within your body. So learn to take deep breaths and start exhaling them slowly. Pay extra attention to how well you can feel your lungs expand, how much air you can

draw in one breath, without over-exerting yourself. Practice holding your breath for some time and then exhaling it slowly instead of in one go or in a rush.

Asanas for Beginners

Without further ado, let's get started with the asanas.

The Mountain Pose – One of the simplest asanas, all you need to do is:

1. On the end of your yoga mat, stand erect, without any hunches or bends in the knees. Once you stand as tall and straight as you can, facing the sun, keep your shoulders relaxed. Spread your body weight as evenly as possible on both your feet and let you arms hang freely but not over-limply at your sides.

2. Draw a deep breath in and raise slowly raise your arms over your head, fingers fully extended. Once your arms are fully raised, make a conscious effort to keep them fully stretched without any bends at the elbows and with your breath drawn in.

Hold the pose and your breath for as long as you can.

3. Gently bring your arms down, exhaling slowly while do doing so. Repeat this asana as many times as you want.

The Inverted Dog Pose – This is one asana that you may have done inadvertently done many times while you were playing with your kid or when you just wanted to stretch some of your stiff limbs. What differs this from a casual stretch is the way you monitor and regulate your breathing and the number of sets of you that are included in this asana.

1. On a clean yoga mat, be on all your fours so that your arms are bent under your shoulders, your face is close to the mat and you your calves are bent at the knees. Keep your hand's palms down on the mat, fingers fully outstretched and your toes also fully stretched.

2. Push your arms forward slowly; glide them over the mat while your elbows brush across it. Let your fingers remain outstretched.

3. When you pushed your arms forward a bit, slowly start raising your hips upwards. Lift your hips as high as possible. When you have done so to the maximum, you will realise that your arms and legs are fully stretched and your body as formed an inverted V shape.

4. Keep your shoulder away from your ears so that too are fully extended laterally. Your feet should be little apart too so that you can stretch to the maximum limit in all limbs.

5. Retain this pose for 3 full, slow inhalations and exhalation.

The Warrior Pose – This is another simple pose which when done repeatedly works wonders on your body's posture and balancing skills. So here is how you do this asana:

1. Place your feet about 3 to 4 feet apart. Make sure your right foot is placed in such a manner that it is at 90 degrees with the rest your body and your left foot is slightly turned in to retain your balance.

2. Gently bring your arms to your hips and then raise them fully. Extend both arms fully from the shoulders and keep your palms facing down.

3. To complete the asana, bend your right knee slightly while you keep your left foot fully stretched and your body slightly turned towards

your right. Hold this pose for a minute while you deeply breathe in and out.

4. Return to your original position and repeat the asana in the opposite direction. Keep switching sides and repeat this asana a few times.

The Tree Pose – Another pose that can help you a lot with your balance, posture and overall blood circulation, this may be a teeny-tiny bit difficult to master in the first few attempts. But once you do, you will be tempted to do this often because it helps you relax so well.

1. Stand erect on the mat with your arms loosely held at your sides.

2. Place your entire body weight on your left leg while you slowly start taking your right leg off the ground. Once it is off, bring the sole of your right leg in contact with the inner thigh of your left leg which is now firmly planted on the mat and bearing your full body weight.

3. When you have so adjusted your feet and body weight, gently bring your arms in front of you, fully outstretched, in a namaskar (palms placed together).

4. When you take your next deep breath after you have so arranged your limbs, bring your hands above your head, fully outstretched and palms facing each other. Retain this final pose for at least 30 seconds while you keep focussing on your breathing.

5. Gently bring your arms back to your sides and bring your right foot back on the mat. Repeat the ritual with your right foot on the mat and your left foot folded inwards at the knee.

6. You will face some issues in balancing your complete body weight on just one foot but the key is in keeping the foot firmly planted and your toes fully outstretched.

The Bridge Pose – It's not often you get a chance you stretch your torso and give some exercise to your spine. Doing so aggressively will certainly hurt them but with this asana, you are achieving the good results without any bad side effects.

1. Lie on the mat with your feet close together and your arms placed firmly on your sides. All limbs should be fully outstretched and your palms must be facing downwards on the mat.

2. Keep an inverted v with both your feet; bring your knee up with your soles planted on the mat. You should, however, bring them up in such a manner that your feet are not bent at the hips. Bring your feet apart a couple of feet.

3. Your hands should continue to remain on your sides but now fisted and resting on their sides. Make sure the sides facing the exterior (away from the rest of your body) are resting on the mat, from shoulder to fisted palms.

4. Raise your hip and chest once your arms and feet are so placed. When you have raised them off the ground fully, your head, arms, feet soles will remain firmly planted on the mat while the rest of the body is placed as much parallel to the ground as possible. Remember – your body weight is now balance on those points that remain on the mat so be careful not to overstrain yourself in this asana.

5. Keeping your chin close to your chest will surely help you. Hold the final pose for a minute and

regulate your breathing pattern as much as possible.

6. If you are finding it difficult to get your hip and chest off the mat initially, then you could start off with placing some cushions under your tailbone (the lower end of your spine) so that you find it easier to do the full lift. With the passage of time, you shouldn't need those cushions anymore.

The Triangle Pose–This is another asana that will help you keep your limbs limber while also retain flexibility at your hips.

1. Stand with your feet about 3 feet apart and your arms loosely held at your sides.

2. Bend towards your right while keeping both your legs fully stretched. Do not bend either knee

and continue facing upwards. Your right arms should be fully extended and placed as close to your right knee as possible while your left arm is held as high above as possible, palm down.

3. Inhale and exhale 5 times while to continue to retain this pose.

4. Switch sides and repeat this asana. Do a few sets of this asana with both sides exercised, as much as possible.

The Seat with a Twist – This is one of the most beneficial asanas for those who are suffering from hanging bellies and who complain of stiff shoulders and backs often. With the help of this asana, one can easily tone their stomach muscles while they stretch their arms fully and feet to a certain extent. It is also useful for the strengthening of your body obliques.

1. Sit on the mat and extend your feet in front of you fully.

2. Bring your right foot under your left thigh so that your right knee is bent, the sole is facing outwards and it is placed directly under the end of your left thigh (at the junction between your thigh and your hip). Continue keeping your left leg fully extended on top of your folded right leg.

3. Now, bring your left leg over your folded right leg. Place it with the left sole firmly placed on the mat near the bent right knee so that forms an inverted V.

4. Keep your torso turned towards the left while right arms are placed on the left leg which is now

in the shape of an inverted V. Your right arm must be placed as far behind your body as possible while your back remains upright, palm facing downwards on the mat.

5. Hold this pose for 3-4 minutes and then switch sides and repeat same motions.

The Cobra Asana – Remember how this powerful snake rises to a challenge? Its tail portion remains coiled or firmly on the ground while it slowly raises only its head and then it's middle section? This is exactly how you will be lying on the mat once you have completed this asana. Needless to say, it strengthens your forearms and helps in stretching your spine.

1. Lie on your stomach on the yoga mat. Your arms must be bent at the elbows and the palms must be facing downwards, with the finger lying under your chin.

2. Your feet must be fully stretched and the toes must be lying on the mat (inverted), heel facing upwards.

3. Slowly raise your head and then your stomach so that your hip is just off the ground. Remember to tighten your glutes while your hip is off the ground.

4. Keep your shoulder straight and place your body weight mostly on your arms, which would be almost fully extended, only slightly bent at the elbows. Try and slowly raise your palms too so that you are ultimately balancing only on your fingertips and your inverted toes.

5. Hold this pose for 3-4 minutes and then return to original position. Repeat this asana a few times.

The Camel Pose – This is one for you to tame your lower abdomen muscles and also exercise your feet and soles.

1. Place knees on the mat while you sit upright. Your soles should be facing up.

2. Slowly start bending backwards and place your palms on your soles. Bend as much as you can while remaining upright.

3. Inhale and exhale deeply while you do this asana.

The Child's Pose – Arguably one of the easiest poses, this is known to help improve circulation of blood to the head and also relax your body while you also exercise your limbs.

1. Sit on the mat in such a manner that your knees are bent, your toes are lying on the mat and you are leaning forward.

2. Lace your chest on your bent knees fully and stretch your arms fully in front of you, palm down.

3. Place your head comfortably between your arms on the mat and breath deeply.

The important thing to note before you begin with these asanas is that you should consult your physician or specialist doctor. This is because they will let you know if you can do these asanas or which are permitted and which are restricted. As there are a lot of internal changes that take place, they may lead to sudden changes in the way some of your internal organs function. Therefore, they may lead to complications if you suffer from illnesses of major internal organs.

Yoga Asanas to Help with Weight Loss, Stress and Pain Relief

Yoga is known to have multifold benefits. It can be seen as a holistic package that aims at rejuvenating and cleansing the body from outside and within. In additional to this, it can help get rid of stress and bring about weight loss. So, let's look at some of the poses that help achieve this:

The Crescent Pose

1. Assume the pose that would in the Mountain Pose and bend your right knee forward.

2. Drag your left foot back so that it rests on the toes and it is fully extended in the reverse direction.

3. Keep your torso upright and your arms to the sides of your head.

4. Now. Slowly start curving your back so that your face is fully facing upwards and your back is pulled as low as you possibly can without losing your balance. Ensure your arms are now joined at the palms in a simple namaskar or with fingers interlocked while the two forefingers are outright and firmly pressed together. This will cause you to bend your right knee a little more but your left foot should continue to remain fully outstretched.

The Boat Pose

1. Lie fully on your back with your knees close together and your arms firmly by your side.

2. Lift your legs off the mat while still joined at the knees and toes. At the same time, start raising your torso and head off the ground.

3. Your arms must be raised so that they are straight and palms are facing upwards at an angle with the ground.

4. Your body weight will be completely on the hip which is the only part of your body that will remain the mat.

The beauty of these asanas and the rest of them explained earlier is that they all work in easing various aches in the body and also help with the reduction of stress.

There are a few reasons why these miraculous changes happen:

1. Your bones are joined with each other at the socket and these contain some fluid with them. With the passage of time and lack of adequate activity, the amount of this fluid (synovial fluid) is reduced which causes a lot of discomforts when

we try to move our limbs or even worse, the bones start grinding against each other. Yoga ensures that this fluid is never lost due to inactivity.

2. Sometimes, there is an inadequate amount of blood supplied to certain parts of our body because they lie unused or pressed against a surface for a really long time, especially our backs and lower backs. These are the main areas of pain and with the help of yoga, you are exercising them thus causing fewer aches. More blood circulation to all body parts means they function fully and without any hiccups. Interestingly, blood circulation is majorly impacted by the slow inhalation and exhalation cycles that you maintain while performing all the asanas.

3. As you can see from the asanas above, many of them ensure blood also passes to the brain in an adequate manner. With the proper circulation of blood to the brain, reduction of pain, and adequate

exercising of body parts, the mind is less susceptible to stress.

4. Keeping your entire body exercised means there is more fat burnt. You lose not just unnecessary weight but also get rid of the flab off your body. Lesser body weight also leads to a more active life, unclogged blood vessels, more stamina and of course, a big boost to the mind in terms of self-respect because you start looking better and you feel fitter.

Getting Started with Meditation

Mindset and benefits explained in detail in this and next chapter. Most of the steps to be taken to start meditating in the right manner have already been discussed when we explained about getting started with yoga asanas. But below is a comprehensive list of the all the steps.

1. Paraphernalia – The only thing you really need to get started with meditation is a good object to sit on. Some of you may prefer sitting on the floor but for those of you who don't, who have health issues preventing them from doing so or who prefer meditating for long hours, there are other options like yoga mats, cushions, a low meditation chair or bench.

2. Timer – It is important to get used to the right amount of meditation and so that you don't lose a track of time while you are lost in meditation, keep an alarm nearby. When you have meditated

sufficiently, your body will form an inbuilt alarm that will let you know when you need to stop meditating.

3. Attire – You don't have to perform any physical activities – pulls, bends, stretched, curls, contortions, lunges, etc., so all you need to do is ensure you have good comfortable clothes.

The Posture

1. Now that you have the right things with you, the next important thing you need to focus on when it comes to meditating is sitting comfortably on the mat or cushion with your back fully upright.

2. Keeping your eyes would be preferable as it helps you shut out distractions more effectively and also soothes your mind and body.

3. It is preferable to form a circle with your index finger and thumb and place your arms stretched on your folded knees as it helps a lot with

concentration. Those who have meditated often can even skip this and just place them palms facing downwards with their arms outright on their knees, though not very rigidly.

4. Crossing your legs is preferable as this again helps with concentration. Some people place both soles facing upwards on the opposite legs thigh.

The Process and Mindset

Once you have assumed the right posture, start your timer and get started with meditation. Here are some helpful tips about meditating right:

1. Keep yourself comfortable on the mat and shut off your phone.

2. Start focussing on your breathing pattern. This is the central point of meditation and focussing on the way you draw your breath, how long you hold it in and exhaling as slowly as you can help you remain

focussed completely on this and shutting off external distractions.

3. Force yourself to completely stop thinking. Picturing a blank, white screen should help you achieve this state of no mental blankness.

4. Do not let your mind wander. Even if you need up thinking about something else, force your mind to revert to this state of blankness and continue breathing in and out slowly.

5. Meditate every day, even if it is only for 15-20 minutes.

6. Begin meditating for a short duration and then extend it for as long as you can.

7. Do not confuse meditation with hypnotism or sleeping.

8. Meditate in a place that is as quiet as you can possibly find so that you have no distractions.

The Benefits of Yoga and Meditation

While there are several benefits that have been documented so far and much more that are being discovered, here are some of the most important and necessary benefits that you should know and which can get you to start these good practices as quickly as possible:

1. Improves muscle strength and tautness

2. Improves your posture when you sit and stand

3. Helps retain the bone bonds strong and bone quality even during the later years of your life

4. Keeps your spine flexible and protected.

5. Improves blood circulation to all parts of the body.

6. Helps in the training of unnecessary fluids from the lymph nodes and gives a major boost to our immunity system.

7. Regulates our heart beats, if done correctly and without over-exerting ourselves.

8. Helps in the regulation of blood pressure, especially by lowering high blood pressure.

9. Helps in the proper functioning of our adrenalin glands.

10. Reduces stress drastically thus leaving us cheerful and positive at all times.

11. Helps lower blood sugar.

12. Stronger mental functions mean we can retain memories longer and better and in focussing on important things.

13. Keeps our internal organ systems smoothly functioning and relaxed.

14. Keeps our nervous system in good order.

15. You can sleep deeper and better with the help of regular yoga.

16. Ups the performance of our lungs.

17. Gradually causes body pain, especially in the joints and muscles to disappear.

18. Helps with self-esteem and reconnecting with our inner selves.

19. You are encouraged and energised to take care of yourself better and at all times.

20. Much better body flexibility; all over.

The 7 Day Yoga Program

As a BONUS here is a short yoga program briefly described that can be your definitive plan to get started with. Take an action, because action changes things!

DAY 1

Getting warmed up – Begin with the breathing exercise. You could start your routine by including meditation and then warming up your body with simple stretched and including the Dog and the Mountain Pose.

The Mountain Pose – One of the simplest asanas, all you need to do is:

1. On the end of your yoga mat, stand erect, without any hunches or bends in the knees. Once you stand as tall and straight as you can, facing the sun, keep your shoulders relaxed. Spread your body weight as evenly as possible on both your feet and let you arms hang freely but not over-limply at your sides.

2. Draw a deep breath in and raise slowly raise your arms over your head, fingers fully extended. Once your arms are fully raised, make a conscious effort to keep them fully stretched without any bends at the elbows and with your breath drawn in. Hold the pose and your breath for as long as you can.

3. Gently bring your arms down, exhaling slowly while do doing so. Repeat this asana as many times as you want.

See the image of this pose in chapter 5 -Asanas for beginners.

The Inverted Dog Pose – This is one asana that you may have done inadvertently done many times while you were playing with your kid or when you just wanted to stretch some of your stiff limbs. What differs this from a casual stretch is the way you monitor and regulate your breathing, and the number of sets of you that are included in this asana.

1. On a clean yoga mat, be on all your fours so that your arms are bent under your shoulders, your face is close to the mat and you your calves are bent at the knees. Keep your hand's palms down on the mat, fingers fully outstretched and your toes also fully stretched.

2. Push your arms forward slowly; glide them over the mat while your elbows brush across it. Let your fingers remain outstretched.

3. When you pushed your arms forward a bit, slowly start raising your hips upwards. Lift your hips as high as possible. When you have done so to the maximum, you will realise that your arms and legs are fully stretched and your body as formed an inverted V shape.

4. Keep your shoulder away from your ears so that too are fully extended laterally. Your feet should be little apart too so that you can stretch to the maximum limit in all limbs.

5. Retain this pose for 3 full, slow inhalations and exhalations.

See the image of this pose in chapter 5 -Asanas for beginners.

DAY 2

Begin with the breathing exercise and warming up your body with simple stretching. Once your body has limbered up, you can graduate to Tree Pose while you also include meditation.

The Tree Pose – Another pose that can help you a lot with your balance, posture and overall blood circulation, this may be a teeny-tiny bit difficult to master in the first few attempts. But once you do, you will be tempted to do this often because it helps you relax so well.

1. Stand erect on the mat with your arms loosely held at your sides.

2. Place your entire body weight on your left leg while you slowly start taking your right leg off the ground. Once it is off, bring the sole of your right leg in contact with the inner thigh of your left leg which is now firmly planted on the mat and bearing your full body weight.

3. When you have so adjusted your feet and body weight, gently bring your arms in front of you, fully outstretched, in a namaskar (palms placed together).

4. When you take your next deep breath after you have so arranged your limbs, bring your hands above your head, fully outstretched and palms facing each other. Retain this final pose for at least 30 seconds while you keep focussing on your breathing.

5. Gently bring your arms back to your sides and bring your right foot back on the mat. Repeat the ritual with your right foot on the mat and your left foot folded inwards at the knee.

6. You will face some issues in balancing your complete body weight on just one foot but the key is in keeping the foot firmly planted and your toes fully outstretched.

See the image of this pose in chapter 5 -Asanas for beginners.

DAY 3

Begin with the breathing exercise and warming up your body with simple stretching. Switch to the Warrior Pose with meditation.

The Warrior Pose – This is another simple pose which when done repeatedly works wonders on your body's posture and balancing skills. So here is how you do this asana:

1. Place your feet about 3 to 4 feet apart. Make sure your right foot is placed in such a manner that it is at 90 degrees with the rest your body and your left foot is slightly turned in to retain your balance.

2. Gently bring your arms to your hips and then raise them fully. Extend both arms fully from the shoulders and keep your palms facing down.

3. To complete the asana, bend your right knee slightly while you keep your left foot fully stretched and your body slightly turned towards your right. Hold this pose for a minute while you deeply breathe in and out.

4. Return to your original position and repeat the asana in the opposite direction. Keep switching sides and repeat this asana a few times.

See the image of this pose in chapter 5 -Asanas for beginners.

DAY 4

Begin with the breathing exercise and warming up your body with simple stretching. Assume the Bridge Pose with shorter meditation.

The Bridge Pose – It's not often you get a chance you stretch your torso and give some exercise to your spine. Doing so aggressively will certainly hurt them but with this asana, you are achieving the good results without any bad side effects.

1. Lie on the mat with your feet close together and your arms placed firmly on your sides. All limbs should be fully outstretched and your palms must be facing downwards on the mat.

2. Keep an inverted v with both your feet; bring your knee up with your soles planted on the mat. You should, however, bring them up in such a manner that your feet are not bent at the hips. Bring your feet apart a couple of feet.

3. Your hands should continue to remain on your sides but now fisted and resting on their sides. Make sure the sides facing the exterior (away from the rest of your body) are resting on the mat, from shoulder to fisted palms.

4. Raise your hip and chest once your arms and feet are so placed. When you have raised them off the ground fully, your head, arms, feet soles will remain firmly planted on the mat while the rest of the body is placed as much parallel to the ground as possible. Remember – your body weight is now balance on those points that remain on the mat so be careful not to overstrain yourself in this asana.

5. Keeping your chin close to your chest will surely help you. Hold the final pose for a minute and regulate your breathing pattern as much as possible.

6. If you are finding it difficult to get your hip and chest off the mat initially, then you could start off with placing some cushions under your tailbone (the lower end of your spine) so that you find it easier to do the full lift. With the passage of time, you shouldn't need those cushions anymore

.

See the image of this pose in chapter 5 -Asanas for beginners.

DAY 5

Begin with the breathing exercise and warming up your body with simple stretching. The Twisted Seat Pose with meditation.

The Seat with a Twist – This is one of the most beneficial asanas for those who are suffering from hanging bellies and who complain of stiff shoulders and backs often. With the help of this asana, one can easily tone their stomach muscles while they stretch their arms fully and feet to a certain extent. It is also useful for the strengthening of your body obliques.

1. Sit on the mat and extend your feet in front of you fully.

2. Bring your right foot under your left thigh so that your right knee is bent, the sole is facing outwards and it is placed directly under the end of your left thigh (at the junction between your thigh and your hip). Continue keeping your left leg fully extended on top of your folded right leg.

3. Now, bring your left leg over your folded right leg. Place it with the left sole firmly placed on the mat near the bent right knee so that forms an inverted V.

4. Keep your torso turned towards the left while right arms are placed on the left leg which is now in the shape of an inverted V. Your right arm must be placed as far behind your body as possible while your back remains upright, palm facing downwards on the mat.

5. Hold this pose for 3-4 minutes and then switch sides and repeat same motions.

See the image of this pose in chapter 5 -Asanas for beginners.

DAY 6

Begin with the breathing exercise and warming up your body with simple stretching. The Triangle Pose with longer meditation periods.

The Triangle Pose–This is another asana that will help you keep your limbs limber while also retain flexibility at your hips.

1. Stand with your feet about 3 feet apart and your arms loosely held at your sides.

2. Bend towards your right while keeping both your legs fully stretched. Do not bend either knee and continue facing upwards. Your right arms should be fully extended and placed as close to your right knee as possible while your left arm is held as high above as possible, palm down.

3. Inhale and exhale 5 times while to continue to retain this pose.

4. Switch sides and repeat this asana. Do a few sets of this asana with both sides exercised, as much as possible.

See the image of this pose in chapter 5 -Asanas for beginners.

DAY 7

Begin with the breathing exercise and warming up your body with simple stretching. The Child's Pose and meditation.

The Child's Pose – Arguably one of the easiest poses, this is known to help improve circulation of blood to the head and also relax your body while you also exercise your limbs.

1. Sit on the mat in such a manner that your knees are bent, your toes are lying on the mat and you are leaning forward.

2. Lace your chest on your bent knees fully and stretch your arms fully in front of you, palm down.

3. Place your head comfortably between your arms on the mat and breath deeply.

See the image of this pose in chapter 5 -Asanas for beginners.

Good Job!

You are on the best way to live a happier life.

Conclusion

Yoga cannot be considered as just a practice. It is a science – science of integrating mind, body and soul. It is quite important for our overall health as well as well-being as it helps keep various troubles at bay. If one chooses to adopt yoga as a part of his day to day routine, one can feel and see the difference – physically, mentally and spiritually.

Look around you and you will several people who have many physical and mental illnesses that they are trying to beat with a lot of expensive and often harmful chemicals. But turn the other side and you will find some other people enjoying sun-kissed skin baths every morning, a fresh face and body with a cheerful smile on their face all the time, all without chemicals! Try yoga and see which of these groups you belong to – you surely will be a part of the happiness!

This is right time for you to be happy!

After many conversations with my friends and family members, I decided to improve this book and add some value for you today! Many people are struggling in life not even realizing that the big reason for it is their relationship! The only way how to find your peace is to improve yourself in your self-love and love others as well. I think that the TRUST is extremely important for every relationship and that is the reason why you can read bonus chapter right now and start your happier life today!

!!!BONUS!!! Building Trust

No relationship today – marriage or otherwise – can survive without the depth of trust and the power that it brings to the table. Without trust, no relationship will ever be secure enough to continue on for any longer than the first breakdown in communication or trust. So, how do you get around this? How do you avoid these problems from being created in the first place?

Building trusts we all about making sure you can give people the help they need to feel themselves around you. By removing insecurities and personal worries in a person you can create something that ensures you can have fun together whilst having genuine fun.

What do we mean by this? It's actually quite simple; too many people make the foolish mistake of building trust on a superficial life. Trust goes a lot further than not being with someone else whilst you are married; it comes down to a lot more than that. No, trust is built upon the fact that you know every single that your wife or husband can count on you to be there for them at all times.

You can be seen as the dependable one; the one who can think of solutions in tight situations. The one who can see the way forward through a problem when there looks to be the solution in sight. Most importantly, though, trust lets your other half be themselves without having to worry about what you will think.

The trust in a relationship is what lets both parties be unapologetically themselves. This is a good thing as having that kind of extra belief in yourself because of a loved one is such a powerful thing. By delivering this kind positive feeling into your relationship, you quickly make sure that you both understand one another and that you have no problems about the fact that there are differences in opinion and belief amongst you both.

So, how do you build trust in one another?

Never belittle their achievements or their personality quirks. This is a very easy way to send someone back into their shell and not only mistrust you but the whole work.

Always give someone the time to get their opinions and ideas across, even if you disagree with the sentiment. Make sure they can feel comfortable expressing themselves, even if you have a debate afterward. Always keep debates healthy and friendly, so they can feel further confidence.

Take the time needed to understand where they are coming from on a range of subjects. By having a greater idea of the ideological spectrum of your partner, it makes communication much easier to control and manage moving forward here.

The last major factor of success here is going to come from being able to help them through their fears. You don't need to have the answers – you just need to have the empathy to listen and provide them with comfort. Trust is not just staying faithful – it's about letting both parties grow together.

If You Enjoyed This Chapter You Can Find More In Full Ebook Right on Amazon.com search for **MARRIAGE**: Quick Advice How To Solve Your Problems In Relationship, Improve Communication Skills, Trust And Guide Your Marriage To Love, Intimacy And Happiness.

Best of luck!

Anna Shine

Made in the USA
Middletown, DE
03 February 2018